MELLIFLUOUS
(SWEET AND SMOOTH, PLEASING TO HEAR)

Linda Jay

First published by Busybird Publishing 2022

Copyright © 2022 Linda Jay

ISBN: 978-1-922954-07-7

This book is copyright. Apart from any fair dealing for the purposes of study, research, criticism, review, or as otherwise permitted under the Copyright Act, no part may be reproduced by any process without written permission. Enquiries should be made through the publisher.

This is a work of fiction. Any similarities between places and characters are a coincidence.

Cover design: Busybird Publishing

Layout and typesetting: Busybird Publishing

Busybird Publishing
2/118 Para Road
Montmorency, Victoria
Australia 3094
www.busybird.com.au

Who is Linda Jay?

Linda grew up in the Adelaide Hills, on a self-sufficiency farm/donkey farm. When her parents separated, she moved down the hill with her mum, but suburban life was to her, like water is to a cat. Shortly afterwards she started working backstage in theatre and rock and roll, and while still a teenager, began touring with bands and theatre shows around the country. There were very few females working backstage in the industry at that time, but the challenges of set construction and roady work was something that she loved.

This work has taken her to many places, and shown her a great diversity of life.

Linda has always been creative, and both a writer and performer from very young. She has seized any opportunity to wear a costume, be theatrical, dance and entertain others.

Eventually her love of theatre and poetry combined, and she began performing her poetry at folk festivals all across the country. For awhile she shifted between performing and backstage, often integrating the two during her time in circus and the Spiegeltent. She even added her love for animals when her cheeky, spotted pony, Rocky, joined her as another element of performance and atmosphere. This pony is now retired and still lives with her on the farm. During her travels, Linda taught herself guitar and banjo as another way to carry her words to audiences through song.

Her reputation in the backstage entertainment work kept her very busy, and this side of her life took over for a while…. and then, in the twists of life… she had some pretty thick sludge and rough hurdles to get over for a while… and now re-emerging as both a writer and performer, presenting her works through poetry and song.

Linda resides on a beautiful property in the Yarra Ranges, surrounded by magnificent mountain views, rivers and donkeys. As soon as she had acreage, she went back to her childhood love of donkeys. Here she breeds, trains and rescues donkeys. She teaches people about donkeys, and provides donkeys for film, TV and events. Also donkeys for therapy and farm stay.

In her writing, Linda often uses the images of nature to express the emotions that we feel as people.

Yesterday a young man was camped on my pasture. He spent the whole day staring at the mountains with a note book on his lap.

When I checked on him in the afternoon he said he was a writer, looking for inspiration.

When I told him I write, he said,

"How do you start? How do you write?"

HOW DO I WRITE?

It rises out of me like the transpiration on those hills.
It curls around my hair and drips onto my shoulders
with the quenching of summer rain.
It rolls around my ears, ringing like echoes over a mountain.
It sings in my eyes and then washes over my brain in colours.
It tangles into my thoughts and sinks into my heart.
Where it aches as it goes deeper.
I hold onto it there… where it stirs through my emotions.
Then it flows through my blood, and beats in my centre.
It seeps out of my skin and dances on the hairs of my arms,
Before trickling down my fingertips and into my pen.
How do I write?
I actually don't know 🥲
I guess I just allow myself to feel.

SAND PICTURES

My fingers are cold
As they push through the sand,
But my images are bold
As they draw who I am.

Nearing completion,
The tide washes in,
Sinking the sketches,
Swashing and levelling.

The sea takes my image,
But she leaves a clean slate.
The sand stays the same,
It just changes shape.

To cause no impact,
but releasing expression,
I change my environment
Without leaving an impression.

My pretty pictures,
may be washed away,
but I amused myself,
and I liked it that way.

It might have been nice
to show someone else,
but the person who needed
to see was myself.

SEA BUBBLE

She drifted slowly from the bottom,
The current twisted her at first.
The spiral pushed her upwards
And she accelerated from the earth.

Where had this bubble come from?
Air in a liquified land.
She wasn't flooded by the world around her,
But used it to lift and expand

Was she the product of flourishing seaweed?
A molusc pushing through sand?
The burp of a bloated fish?
Or shifting of a sideways crab?

Shimmering blue and silver,
She rolled through turbulent water.
She was focused on her destination,
So she missed all those who admired her.

Light shined on the particles suspended,
But none reflected her sparkle.
Attractive in her translucence,
she lured me with her aspirations.

She may have pierced me with a fishhook,
As a thread carried me behind her.
Her oxygen could breathe inside me
If I could pierce her denying ascension.

Afraid by her delicate nature,
Drawn by awe and fascination,
I swam, pursuing her silently,
Captured by wonder and inspiration.

As she neared the surface,
I realised there was no tomorrow.
Overwhelmed by desire and confusion,
I was suddenly filled with sorrow.

Without hesitation she hit her target,
Her skin opened and she became free.
She burst into invisible nothing,
And discovered her reality.

As she approached the boundary,
Did she notice the sky was a mirror?
As she vanished into infinity,
My ocean became instantly clearer.

Although I respect her motivation,
She taught me a valuable lesson.
I will admire all those around me,
And appreciate my own location.

IMPRESSIONS

I begin my journey like the morning sand,
No footprints or scars of where things land.
But with each interaction, an impression is drawn.
I am shaped by the print, but continue on.

Sometimes it's just a ripple, a memory of time,
Beautiful in its shape, and yet just a line.
Sometimes it goes deeper, and fills like a pool,
With a life of its own, filled with prickles or jewels.

Sometimes it is brittle and breaks like a shell,
Or it could be a storm, that's as crazy as hell.
Some shift with the tide, while others remain
A solid impression of pleasure or pain.

Some pause for a moment to look at the shore,
Some camp for a night and need nothing more.
Some sweep a change that is carried for life.
Some are just ships which pass in the night.

Everyone leaves footprints as they run on the sand.
Each indentation shapes who I am.
Some are just shallow, and some are just there,
But some hurt forever in the truths that lay bare.

Is this what life is? Is this what it means?
To evolve with the shapes as it changes the scenes.
When the next tide comes in and a fresh beach is laid,
The old one becomes history as sandstone is made.

ROLLING TRANSIENT

Rolling through the bus of life,
Taking a road through changes.
Attracted by the world outside,
Framed as a series of images.

Looking through the window,
They continue to pass,
The space, the fields and villages.
The depth and width of the open sky,
And the clouds which paint its picture.

Colours subtle and vast,
And bright contrast.
The line between the shadows.
I wave to the face of the unknown place.
They vacantly smile, a stranger.

On the verge of the curve of the road ahead,
Opening frames which show their wonders.
Without touching the wheel, or feeling a peddle,
I let suspension ride over the troubles.

HEADING HOME

Leaving behind the city scrapers,
The bustle and buzz of the traffic.
High speed freeway, a beeline for home.
Windows down, and muzzle to the air,
Lapping up the fond fragrance
Of eucalypts and pines
Taste the trees and the dewy mist,
Crystals cleansing, cool and crisp.
I had forgotten the mystique of massive trees,
Bending, waving, taunting breeze.
Eternal horizons amaze my eyes.
Flowing clouds simmer in an expanse of sky.
Soon we'll be home, by a well stoked fire.
Welcome baked dinner and apple pie.
Stories and laughter bubble the air.
It's good to be home with those who care.

GOOD MORNING

Good Morning
Today I awake to the gentle patter of soft rain drops on the tin.
A welcome sound.
The light is darker, and the air a little cooler than previous mornings,
So it is a little harder to draw myself out of bed.
A weight in the mattress calling "wait and stay a little longer"
Eventually I deny myself.
Extracting my heavy bones from the clutches of the doona to present myself at the entrance of the day.
Even the dogs are stretched out on their lounges,
Preferring a rub on the belly to a bounce at the door.
Outside the air is still,
Motionless except for the trill of bird song.
The sky is grey with its drifting, smoky pictures.
The rain falls lightly.
A refreshing shower, blessing my cheeks and weighing down the curls in my hair.
I linger at the forest edge and breathe in the eucalypts.
The dogs sniff at the trails of last night's adventures.
Paths of creatures who have been and gone in our sleep.
Today I am happy to feel the soft rain on my shoulders and have no desire for a coat.
I welcome the water and the soft light,
And open the gate to start my new day.
Good Morning 🙂

TODAY IN SOLITUDE

The sunrise painted a watercolour,
The bird calls rang in my ears.
The wild dogs bayed in the distance,
Reminding me of our fears.

But the sun came in gold and shining.
Soaking life right into my skin.
Her heat so warm and healing,
It turned a cog wheel within.

The clouds came over so dramatically,
Arriving with a thunder and crash.
My dog headed under for cover,
But I stood where I could watch.

The drops fell heavy in a song of refreshment.
The light hit the silver and shone.
The sound roared on the tin above me,
And the fragrances were soothing the lungs.

Then I remembered things I'd forgotten,
And so I ran out into the shower.
I slowed down to just a walk.
The drenching made me feel empowered.

And then as the evening settled,
And quiet sank over the hills
I found peace in my solitude,
And found place as I stood still.

The fog came in low and beautiful,
And stopped me from seeing beyond.
But I found when I stopped running,
That this was the place I belonged.

RAINBOW

He thinks of me as his rainbow.
A reflection of sunshine that's colourful.
Whenever he sees me, he smiles,
And he always says that I'm beautiful.

His relationship to me is distant,
And always limited to observational.
I glow in the hope that one day,
He will see the full beam without obstacles.

Although I retreat in silence,
And my vibrancy becomes invisible,
My vapour always remains true,
And the dew of my form is still touchable.

But to think of me as his reality,
Is a magic he finds, inconceivable.

He never tries to catch the bow,
So, each time, I fade, undetectable.

Does he think I am too far from his darkness,
To be in his hand, so attainable.
The storm is what makes me shine,
His clouds are the droplets which sparkle.

I would fall into a pot of riches,
If he would dig at the ground I come from.
My fears keep me lucid, transparent,
But caring has each particle twinkle.
In silence I whisper the spell,
But he is looking for solid, substantial.
I guess, in the heat, I disappear,
So I suppose I seem evaporational,
But I will always return in his rain,
For his smile to me is invaluable.

MY BEAUTIFUL SKY

My beautiful sky
Is turbulent like a storm.
Sometimes it is cold,
and sometimes it is warm.

Parts of it glow so strongly,
It radiates my whole world,
But other parts are so dark,
They make my centre swirl.

I watch all of its changes,
As it warns me of the rain.
It tries to be so scary,
But I still love it like a flame.

I face my beautiful sky,
And I am taken by its breeze
I will stand and feel the rain
As it flows through all I see,

Once the storm has finished rumbling,
And the wind has passed me by.
I will still be facing the horizon
And watching my beautiful sky.

THE FLOW OF THE CREEK

My little creek is flowing again.
I can hear it growl from the top of the hill.
A storm has blown my human objects,
Upside-down, side-ways and inside-out.
Strewn like skeletons among fallen bark and branches.
Puddles sprawl the width of the paddock,
Making mirrors of the cloudy sky.
My muddy boots stirring the picture with every step.
A lyrebird calls out and announces our arrival.
Followed by the responses from smaller voices in the trees.
The waterfall roars loud,
and I can hear the rocks shifting under the flow.
Everything is wet and dripping.
My cheeks feel freshened, and are lifting.
The power from this watery change
will re-shape the bed, once again.
The silt and mud disappear,
Old mosses give way to be clear.
Icy water makes my hands feel numb,
but the next season change has begun.

INTO THE STORM

A squall builds before me,
I hear the clouds roaring,
A tameless wind is blustering.

I won't go inside,
Where it's safe and dry,
The turbulent force is detonating.

I'll dance rabid wild,
Like a tantrumming child,
In chaos my joy is the dreaming.

In fiery hot vision,
With whirling collision,
Washed down to a grounding clarity.

I spin through the night,
Which turns wind through my hair.
I absorb in the storm as I fly.

It is a cycle itself,
And the reminder is felt.
The system is disguised as disorderly.

Throw me the rain,
It will wet me again,
And once I am soaked, I'll be saturated.

The wet makes me clean,
A cool rinse of energy,
Change makes the seasons appreciated.

Don't grumble the warning,
I know darkness is coming.
Crack open the grey,
Throw it at me.

THE OAK TREE

The oak tree is looking so golden,
Her leaves glow as she stands in her prime.
The morning light dances around her,
And yet I can't see her shine.

The chill has been blowing around her,
And she does her best to hold on,
But her beautiful, summer shelter
Feels like it's already gone.

She seems so strong and magestic,
But under the bark her centre is hollow.
Each year she grows another layer,
Hoping it will be different tomorrow.

She tries to keep her heart open,
And in Spring it is teaming with life,
But once she gives what can be given,
It all disappears overnight.

Some branches which appear to be strong,
Turn out to be brittle and weak,
Sometimes a cloak of kindness,
Covers a selfish drive underneath.

Sometimes words are just words,
They fall away when you make them a song,
Sometimes you can follow your heart,
Only to find it was wrong.

The morning light rises over the mountain,
And she looks to see what it will bring,
It shines in magnificent colour,
And yet she can't make herself sing.

Sometimes you can have a perfect canvas,
And all the paints to make wonderful art,
But the page stares back at you blankly,
And you just don't know where to start.

A TURNING SEASON

This morning I can feel winter tingling in the air.
The tiny droplets of chill are catching on my light,
and I am reminded that change is inevitable.
But the white of the fog doesn't cloud my mind.
The zing in the air makes it clearer.
The colour in the leaves is starting to turn.
My lush green canopy is becoming golden.
As the colours richen, the days shorten.
I know the warmth of summer will soon be leaving.
What was lush and flourishing, and bringing me shelter,
is starting to loosen on their branches.
As the colours deepen, they also become brittle,
and soon they will be brown and crackling.
Taken by the air of the changing season,
they will be blowing across the hills
and tumbling into their next transition.
But I am not sad.
To hold onto a season is to pass with it.
To live, is to step forward as it rolls away.

As the leaves fall, I am nourished,
And another layer grows around my trunk...
But I still love.
Love the summer that was, Love the winter that approaches
and also love the moments inbetween.
I am careful not to pre-empt the ice.
The clouds are still high and the breeze is still warm.
There is much to appreciate through the narrowing days of turning.

You cannot hold back a river because you like it.
You can either stand on the bank and admire it as it rolls by,
or you can immerse yourself in it,
and cherish every feeling as it passes over you.
I always place myself where I can feel.
Yes, it gets cold sometimes,
But life in the deep end enriches my soul.

THE SHOWERS

When you feel the rain fall upon you,
And trickle down your face like tears.
When you feel the ache, as it cuts into your gullies,
and rubs against your fears.
Remember that showers pass
And the landscape is always freshened.
These ripples flow into a bigger picture,
Where the sting of the flow is lessened.
Little trickles join together,
A brook, a creek, a river.
Without showers nothing can grow,
and the flow needs all types of weather.
Welcome the showers.

THE BREAK

When some of us break, we can't see a way,
We fold, crumble and decay.
But some of us grow, from a depth in the hole,
And we find another way.

We build a dream of what could be,
Much bigger than ourselves.
Way out of reach, it's beyond belief,
Like magic dust and elves.

The dark voice blows, and shows us "No",
Those ideas cannot be reached.
But the big-eyed moon, says "it's just too soon",
"Hold on to the light you see."

The sap is drawn into my fronds,
They reach out to be big and green.
They probably won't grow into the picture I've sewn
But their beauty remains to be seen.

When you hear me sing of big crazy things,
It may be that they won't come true.
But holding on to imagination
is a power that gets me through.

One day I will see what has become of me,
And which things I have achieved.
I won't count the cost of the things I have lost.
I will be happy to be bright and green.

(Two trees broke in the same storm over three years ago... one continues to thrive and blossom... this was my inspiration)

WATERY HEALING

From the top of the hill,
I can hear her roaring,
Like a busy freeway at peak hour.
Under my feet the paddock is trickling a chorus,
as the whole field flows down to join the song,
I am captivated and drawn to follow.
The winding water and broadening puddles
Pulling on my curiosity like a thread.
Taking me down to meet the mighty creek.
Barrelling her way down the gully.
Taking with her anything that tries to be still.
Clearing all of last year's clutter from her banks,
And cutting the new shape for this year's flow.
The storm may make us powerless and disconnected, but here I feel life beginning again. Rinsing away my dependence on anything other than myself and awakening me with her strength.
In drought the land lays bare and hard,
Like a body without a heart.
Dry, silent and empty.
Now the veins are pumping again,
My face rises a smile in the spray from her turbulent tumbling.
I feel invigorated by the power, and inspired by her enthusiasm as she effortlessly changes path to make her way across the mountains.
I breathe in the magic of her mist,
And watching her wildness makes me feel free.

A DIFFICULT ROAD

I don't mind travelling a difficult road,
as long as it is genuine.
There is no point flying down a freeway,
if the path is hollow without truth or meaning.
The difficult road sure has its boulders.
Which make me ache, from my feet to my shoulders.
Sometimes I question the road I travel,
with its hurdles of dirt and gravel.
But then I find detail and heart in its simplicity,
things the flyers don't even catch in their periphery.
Sometimes things open in the quietness of time,
That would be lost if you zoomed on by.
In the rock I see the shimmer,
On a shell, I see the glimmer.
The endurance keeps making me stronger,
so what I find is sure to last longer.
While it hurts to climb the rubble,
I can feel love, soft and subtle.
As I negotiate my way through,
I learn about myself, the world, and you.
Through the aching, I find more depth.
While it's hard, I don't regret.

A REFUELLING BREEZE

Sometimes... even when you live in a place as beautiful as this,
there are times that you still just need to get out and fly.
Feeling the wheels roll on the tar,
and the horizon open out before you...
Blowing out the cobwebs of a cluttered mind.
The wind blowing through your hair, wild and free.
Who wants to be boxed in by stagnant air conditioning,
when the breeze in your face can be an option?
One advantage of a '98 Hilux is those little quarter panel windows
Which can steer the air to make you feel as open as driving topless.
I took a cruise out to see some very long loved friends who I haven't seen in several years. Naturally, it was
like I saw them yesterday, and conversation flowed like a river.
Loosening the details of our stories out of every crevice.
Too soon it was time to hit the road back,
But the drive was just as delicious.
A smile lifted my face,
while the wind freshened my heart.
The horizon opened my perspective,
and my friends warmed my soul.
Worth every drop of fuel. ❤

HELEN'S PORCH

Watching the moon rise from Helen's porch.
A wonderful way to close a special day
Welcoming the cool evening air.
The soft pink reflecting in the dam,
Ducks rippling the mirror as they pass over the water.
Conversation flowing and negotiating over the rocks of life,
Like a river smoothing over spikey edges.
Chortling as it laughs over the obstacles,
And meanders its way into cooler waters.
Cows watching us from the fence,
Staring into our hearts with their rich brown eyes
and drawing love from our centre to surface.
Good friends can talk about anything.
The moon lighting our table and softening our faces,
Rises like the time passes,
and lights the pebble path to steer my way home.

A PAWS TO PONDER

On the porch she likes to ponder,
About all that lies so much further.
When she sits by the banks of the river,
She would watch it flow by forever.
Does she stare at the ripples in wonder?
Or just know there is life swimming under?
She sits still in her contemplation,
while her senses unfold the imagination.
In the morning she stares through the trees,
As they shift and sway and the breeze.
Looking for movement and chatter,
Which is cracked by a kookaburra's laughter.
Her eyes dart through the wild, between roses.
A much closer scene than where her nose is.
Shifting through smells of last night,
Who's paths passed over; so light.
Her ears take her even further,
Sifting through the whistling pasture.
Pointing sharp at the rustle of a mouse,
Or the motive of a long distant shout.
The clunk of my cup tells her that I am done.
She bounces fast, as it's now time to run.
Time for the chores of the day,
And through every step, she will play.

SO WARM

I rest my head on her belly like a pillow.
One arm under her face, the other under her tail.
The television is chatting away,
but we aren't listening.
The fire crackles orange,
and blows it's warmth in our direction.
But the warmth between us is stronger.
Ever stronger.
It is cold outside.
It has been a difficult year.
Her paws have trotted beside me,
Through every hill and dale.
When I have crumpled in my chair
she has pressed her strong paws on my shoulders.
And her wet nose cool upon my cheek.
Her fur has been my handkerchief for many broken tears.
Her eyes have drawn out many smiles from the deep.
Her humour finds laughter in the chaos.
She has such sparkle,
it is hard to believe that she is already older.
Too soon I will be her carer,
as she has surely been mine.
I can't imagine that day being ever,
so best she lives a long, long time.
I rest my head on her belly like a pillow,
and absorb the love in her heart.
So warm.

THE BONFIRE

There is something fabulous about a big bonfire.
The crackle in my ears, the warmth on my face.
The dancing light entertaining my eyes.
I breathe deeply and enjoy the glow.
I am tired and sore, aching all over,
But feeling this fire is an empowering transition.
Knowing that what is burning
is a pile of old dead wood.
Broken branches and history.
Packages of troubles, held closed in boxes,
Sealed with cobwebs and dust.
Tucked away to save facing their contents,
Believing that they were best left undisturbed,
Yet there they were, cluttering my future,
and weighing down my wings.
Leaving no room for fresh joys to grow.
Here they are, faced, piled up, and burning.
I shed a tear, but I am smiling.
I look forward to the ash blowing across the paddock
and the coals melting down to leave a clean slate.
Now I can see into my warehouse,
its walls are strong and the frame stands open,
welcoming a new beginning.
There is no rush to fill it,
Just a space, with no lock or key.
I let it lay still for the dust to settle,
Then the next chapter will have somewhere to be.

AIR IN MY FIRE

Breathing fire in my vision,
You blow on my coals.
They may have gone out,
If they were left to grow cold.

Oxygen on embers,
and my colours glow hot.
Your breeze in a catalyst,
which propels my spark.

Your faith in my future,
In my ability to burn,
Gives me strength to reach out,
And flicker my yearn.

If my flames find the timber,
And I catch something more.
I will give heat and light,
For you to keep warm.

As you blow through your palms,
The red gleams higher.
I will never lose hope,
While there is air in my fire.

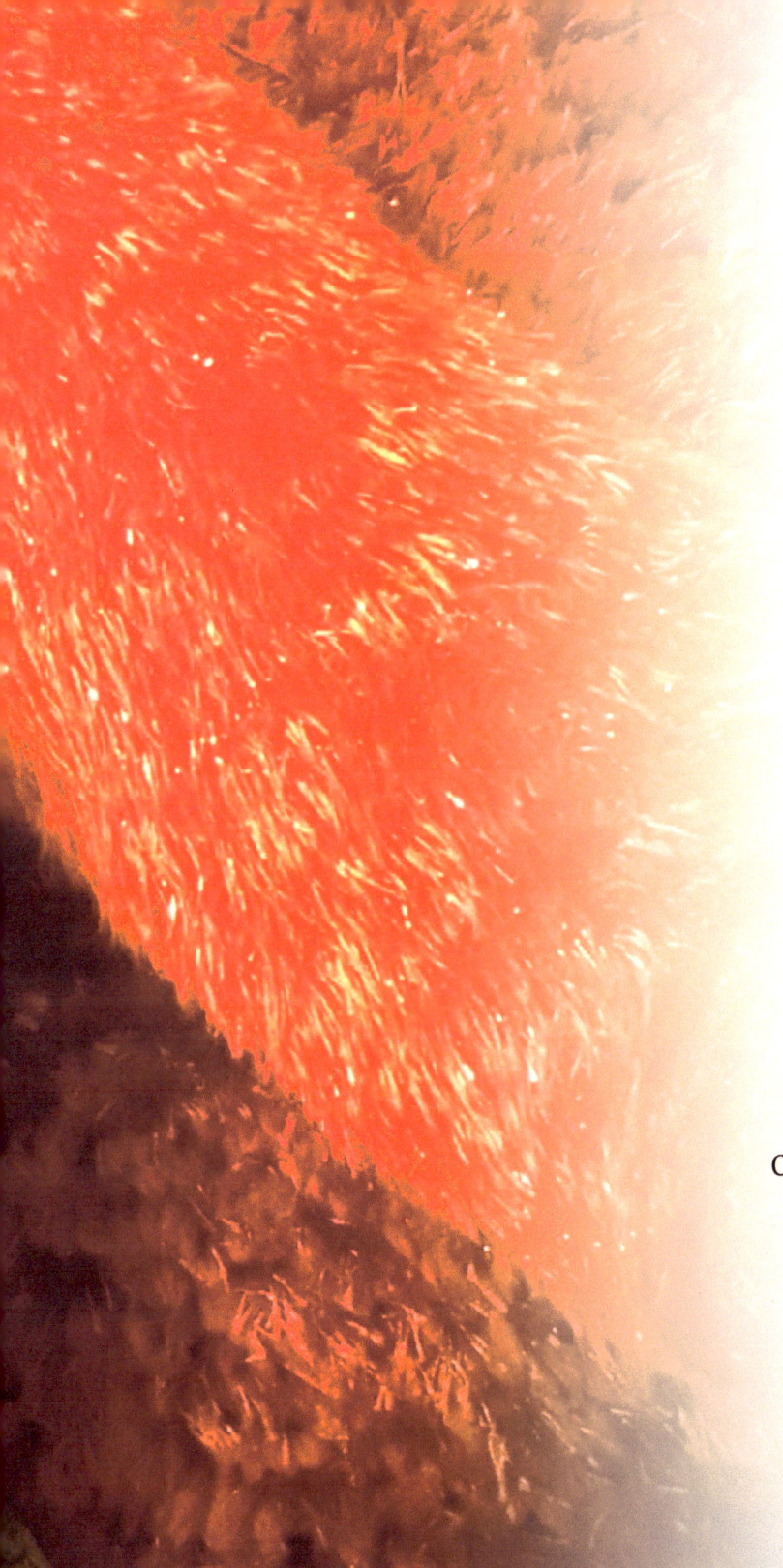

WELCOMING WINTER

Outside the wind whirls and icy spears whip cold through the landscape.
The mountains disappear behind a swirling screen of chilly white.
The creatures are silent as they huddle in their hollows.
The branches are loud as they try to hold on through the battering blows.
I quietly strike a match, and blow a little on the kindling.
My dog moves into position, even though the hearth is still cold.
I place another layer for the flames to climb through
and lay down with my girl to wait.
A hearty soup simmers on the stove, and fluffy scones are freshly baked,
ready to be dipped in the spicey sauce.
A glass of red wine warms on the coffee table.
Not only is it soft and delicious, but it carries my heart
to my friends who grew the grapes and tended the process
so that I can feel this smooth richness on my taste buds.
I listen to another friend's music roll over my ears like a Hawaiian ocean,
Grateful to all of my musical friends,
thoughts take me through laughter and festivals.
My hand feels calmness through my old dog's belly and suddenly I am warm.
Here we are transitioning into winter,
but I am welcoming it like a warm hug after a difficult day.
Curling here on a cosy blanket we rest in the glow and appreciate our shelter. ♥

A MISTY SHROUD

Today I look out,
And the fog's come in.
I can't see beyond the dam.

The white cloak hides
My view of tomorrow,
And I can only see where I am.

My view of the ranges,
Which shows me beyond
The place I stand with my feet.

Is obscured by
A misty shroud,
Hiding the gullies and peaks.

But when I let go
Of what I can't see,
And I am made to see my own space,

I feel the present
For what it is,
Let the beauty of now take shape.

I take a breath in,
And let out a sigh
And the moment shows me its magic.

To miss today
Looking for tomorrow,
Is as common as it is tragic.

Sometimes we let
What may or may not
Stop us from seeing what is.

The shine of wet grass,
Dew on a cobweb,
The light of dawn on the trees.

Moments pass quickly,
But they make the days,
And the days make up the years.

It is easy to miss
The best things in life,
Looking for what might be.

Sometimes a fog,
Returning us home,
Shows us what we really need.

To see the blessings
We hold in our hands,
Free of expectation and greed.

I clear my head
Of its worries and clutter,
I don't even know where that
began.

I can't see past
The here and now,
But it's beautiful where I am.

COLOUR IN THE CHILL

It is 3 degrees outside at the moment,
but fortunately, there is wood on the fire and the house feels warm.
There is an icy chill biting through the air,
but the mountains are painted fairy white.
The rain has been drenching, and everything is soaked and sodden,
but between the clouds, and on top of the snow, there is a rainbow.
The mud is heavy and consuming.
Your feet sinking with every step.
The weight, clinging to where you stand.
Trapping your boots and making it hard to move forward…
but in the mud, there are ducks, wagging their tails with joy,
showing how wonderful it can be with a different perspective.
And in the cold, there are robins.
Clouds of colourful robins,
Enjoying my garden down below the snow-line,
Flitting about between the raindrops,
Painting the brown muck with their vibrant happiness.
In the coldest of days, there are always robins.

FEELING THE FRESH FALL

You couldn't tear the smile from my face,
The doorstep reflecting the glow.
Giggles and squeals take over my sanity,
As I skip and jump in the snow.

Smooth and white, ground in disguise,
The aching chill numbing my toes.
Fairy flakes fall in my hair and eyelashes.
The breezy ice, freezing my nose.

Delicate whisps of vertical grasses,
A picture in black and white.
The leaves hanging heavy, long and laden,
Skeleton trunks alight.

Shadowy figures of sheep and roos,
Ponder, grey, over the hillside.
Warmed by their beauty, I am not at all cold,
As tears well up in my eyes.

A ghostly school bus, winds the road,
Silent seats empty today.
Children learning more at home
As they watch, wallow and play.

Drifting, swirling, settling soft,
These memories will last forever.
Absorb in the magical charm of winter,
And share in this laughter, together.

WINTER SUN

It has been a dark and stormy night.
And my head cracks with pain like lightening.
My body moves like wet concrete,
And I shift in my hollow,
Trying not to let it set hard.
I can see the clouds parting,
And the rays shifting to reveal your blue.
But I am stuck in the weight of a groove.
The air is cold, and the grass is icy all around me.
My feet are bare, and the ground too cold to touch.
My hands ache with the chill, and seek the warmth of a wholesome cup,
And yet I am not brave enough to let them out of my pockets.
I can see the garden opening to your sunshine,
and yet I can't open myself from my covers.
My skin is so thin, and my heart so cold,
I cannot emerge until I know the grass is warm and dry.
Seasons come and go,
And even your blue will pass in time.
I try to lift myself out so that I can feel your rays before change shifts us again...
And yet I am stuck
and it feels so cold.

MUD

Trudging through the mud,
And my sodden feet feel heavy,
The soil squelches between my toes,
And that tickles,
Which encourages a weary smile.
The humid air sits thick in my lungs.
I can't breathe,
I almost cry,
But then I see her,
The dragonfly,
And she awakens my weary eyes.

MELTING WINTER

The morning light glows across the mountains,
Casting a new day of dawn over her flanks.
The storm has blown and trees have fallen.
Snow had sealed the forest heart closed.
The life of love slept quiet in the hollows,
But now the ice of winter melts away.
Her bitterness and edge flows into water.
Now bringing life into the gullies.
The aching coldness retreats,
And the numbness of my centre starts to feel again.
The golden glow spreads herself across my mountain,
Completely changing the picture, I have come to know.
Sometimes we try to change the season,
Building our own fire against the cold.
Each day trying to rekindle the warmth,
When in reality it comes with time.
In time the light shifts, colours change,
And love will waken from its winter crevice.
Now to be more than what she was,
For the heart has grown in her Winter hibernation.

EMERGING FROM THE ICE

We hide inside our deep dark cave,
For winter hibernation.
Closed inside the heavy walls,
For safety and insulation.

We wrap ourselves in a cosy cocoon,
And wait for the transition.
But inside the blackened space,
We lose our orientation.

Our brains spin around in circles,
confined by our secure shell.
Getting knotted up in our own narrative yarns,
For in silence there is nothing else.

But with patience and peace, we let go of the noise,
And eventually hear the world.
As we become stronger, the shell becomes thinner,
And we start to feel the warmth.

Peeling away, the black becomes blue,
And through light we can see in colour.
So amazed at what I have found,
I want to share this with another.

But on my own, I see every shape,
Feel the air, and hear it whisper.
The ice is cold, but shines as it melts,
Soon to be welcomed as water.

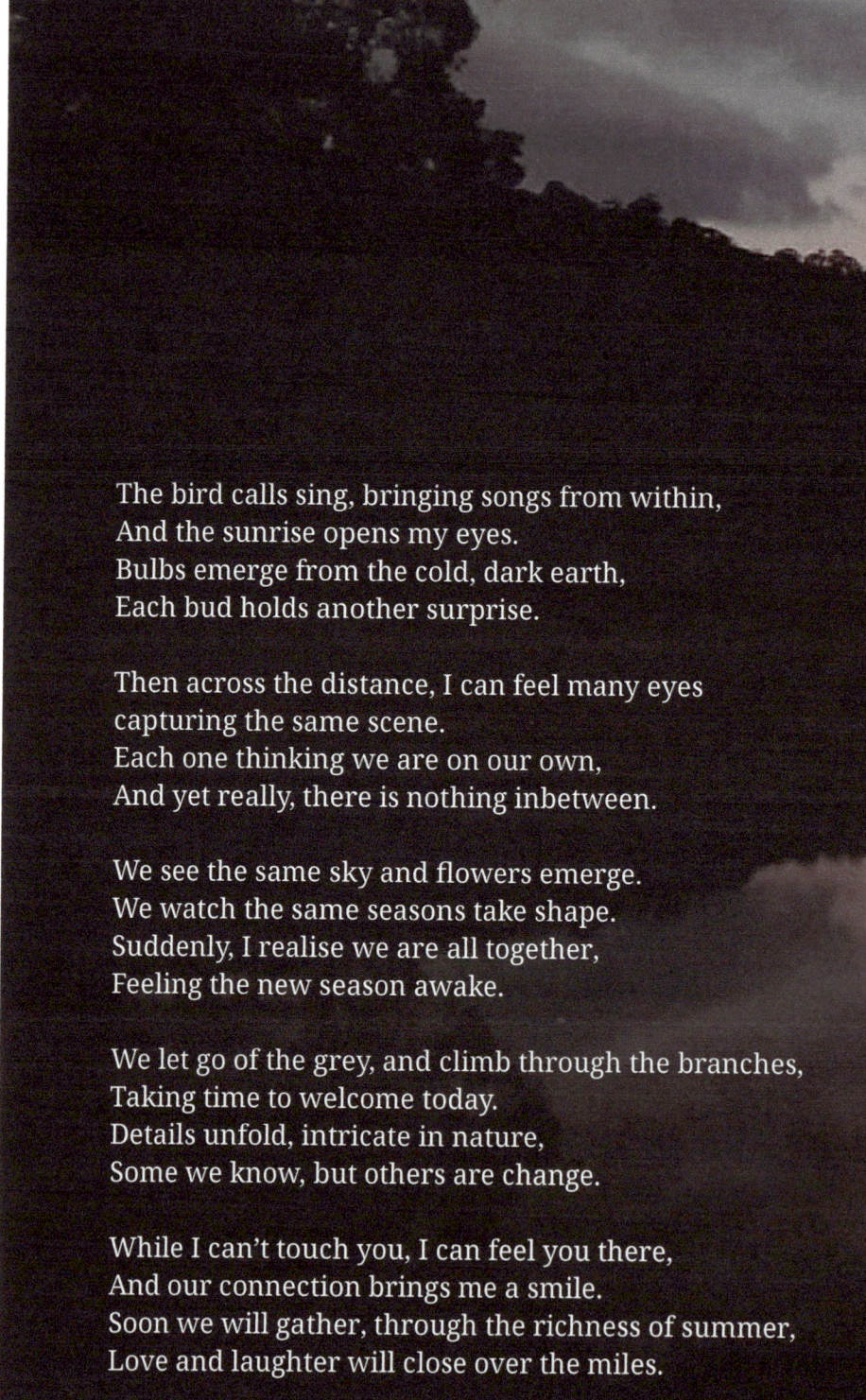

The bird calls sing, bringing songs from within,
And the sunrise opens my eyes.
Bulbs emerge from the cold, dark earth,
Each bud holds another surprise.

Then across the distance, I can feel many eyes
capturing the same scene.
Each one thinking we are on our own,
And yet really, there is nothing inbetween.

We see the same sky and flowers emerge.
We watch the same seasons take shape.
Suddenly, I realise we are all together,
Feeling the new season awake.

We let go of the grey, and climb through the branches,
Taking time to welcome today.
Details unfold, intricate in nature,
Some we know, but others are change.

While I can't touch you, I can feel you there,
And our connection brings me a smile.
Soon we will gather, through the richness of summer,
Love and laughter will close over the miles.

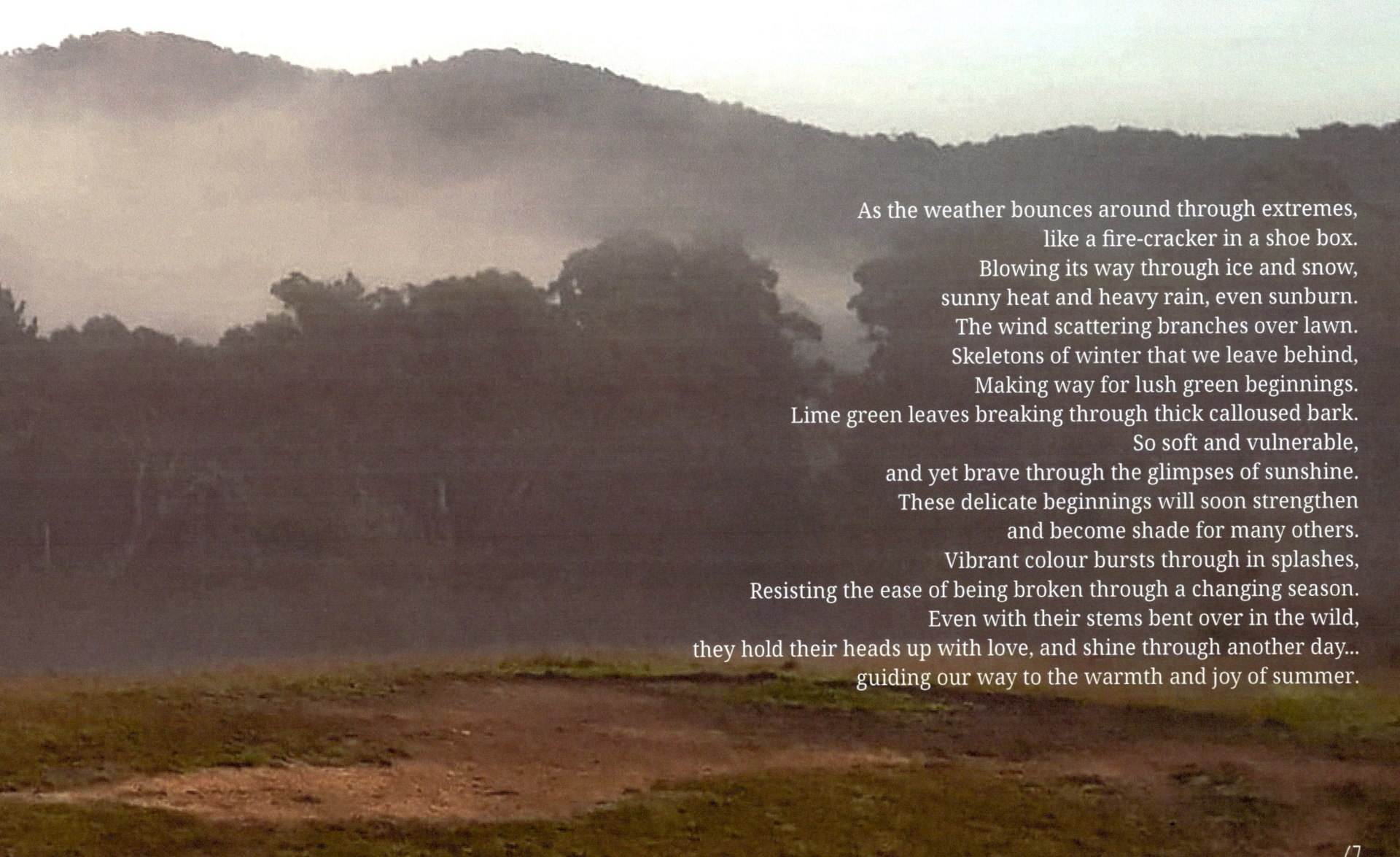

LEAVING WINTER

As the weather bounces around through extremes,
like a fire-cracker in a shoe box.
Blowing its way through ice and snow,
sunny heat and heavy rain, even sunburn.
The wind scattering branches over lawn.
Skeletons of winter that we leave behind,
Making way for lush green beginnings.
Lime green leaves breaking through thick calloused bark.
So soft and vulnerable,
and yet brave through the glimpses of sunshine.
These delicate beginnings will soon strengthen
and become shade for many others.
Vibrant colour bursts through in splashes,
Resisting the ease of being broken through a changing season.
Even with their stems bent over in the wild,
they hold their heads up with love, and shine through another day...
guiding our way to the warmth and joy of summer.

MAGNOLIA

When my branches were like skeletons,
Chilled against an icy sky.
And the wind blew cold through my centre.
I trembled with questions of why.

I stood strong against the harshness of winter
And tried not to freeze into nothing.
While my centre was ringing so hollow,
I knew deep down there was something.

You came to me in a small velvet calyx.
So gentle, soft and sweet.
I shifted my focus to love,
And allowed you to open for me.

The crack in your velvet showed true colours,
And with it you drew out a smile.
Your petals were vibrant and beautiful.
We lingered in hues for awhile.

When I told you, your colour was special,
You insisted you were just a tree.
But I saw a wonderful magic,
That warmed to the heart of me.

The cold winds still weren't over.
They continued to shake and chill.
And heavy rain we weren't expecting,
Bruised more than you were able to give.

The weather became too much for you,
And soon your petals would fall.
I tried so hard to hold on to them,
But some things are beyond all control.

I don't want to let go of your season,
I crave its vibrance and colour.
But some things are meant to pass,
to make way for the new umbrella.

Lush leaves are growing where you were,
And they will shade me through a long, hot Summer.
Through every day they help me grow stronger,
But it's your colours I will remember.

Photo: Melanie Cole

Photo: Helen Valentine

IN A SINGLE DAY

In a single day....
I saw a mother blue wren feeding her young family next to my bird bath.
So close through my kitchen window.
I saw a pair of kingfishers diving into the river while I swam.
My dogs so excited by the water,
they wag their whole bodies over the rapids,
staring into my heart with their love and appreciation.
I found a dainty little nest,
woven into a branch over the protection of flowing water,
It was visited by a cautious white cheeked honey eater.
I had a black cockatoo squeal at his mates
before dropping a Banksia nut on my head.
Laughing to each other as I squalked in my garden.
I felt the temperature drop from hot sizzle to a cool drizzle
as the breeze came in and soothed my face.
I felt the light showers tingle on my arms,
while most evaporated before they hit the ground.
I saw the clouds smoke and the storm light rise,
The trunks and branches glowing like lanterns.
Gold light radiating from every leaf and petal.
I watched the sky darken and then flash,
Cracking its natural light show over the horizon.
I rocked in my garden seat until the storm strengthened,
Taking in the energy of the change,
Trying to resist the need for shelter.
Eventually I curled in my cosy bed,
And just listened.

FLOWERS

Yes, I like yellow daffodils,
In their bold, bright, golden colour.
Punching sunshine into early Spring,
with a "pow" that jumps out of Winter.

They pop loud from the grey, cold shadows,
and dance bright like a show chorus line,
A siren that change is coming,
and warmth will find you in time.

But the flowers I love most,
arrive a little later.
They open quietly in the background,
to bring a soft, gentle picture.

I wait for them to be ready,
As they bring something unique and special.
Complicated in all their ruffles,
Beautiful and yet, so fragile,

Pale until almost transparent,
I can see right into their centre.
A delicate love takes time to grow
But these are the ones I treasure.

A RESILIENT ROSE

Some roses just keep on giving.
In early Spring, when the frosts are icy and heavy,
And uncertainty surrounds the elements.
Opening vulnerable petals holds the risk of bitter chill,
But there between the frozen leaves and white feathers of ice,
she opens her red heart.
Through the joy of warmth and water,
she sings her colour stronger.
As each bloom becomes fragile and falls,
there behind it, opens another.
Through the baking heat of Summer,
The burning fire of sun,
and the wilting thirst of drought,
The wind blowing hot against her stems,
Curling her edges like a furnace.
She stands, stronger and stronger.
And between the scorching rays and dusty dirt,
She holds open her red heart.
In the Autumn, when the rains drench the soil and wash away the sunshine,
and a cold wind blows to the centre.
Icy snow collects on the hill and chills to the core of the garden.
The leaves fall to protect the branches which held them.
No longer able to catch the warmth of sun, which has long gone.
Long after the sustenance of light has past,
and drops catch like tears between the thorns.
She continues to draw scarlet from her roots.
This rose still holds her petals,
And as each one blows apart,
she brings me another, and another
and into the white of winter,
She opens her red centre.

VIOLET'S ROSE

I love the glow of this rose.
It lights like a lantern in a storm.
When the dark grey smothers the mountain,
she brings me a dose of warm.

I have her planted at my entrance,
To lift my heart when I am home.
A welcome arrival of colour,
To bring me back from where I have roamed.

Her picture paints a reminder
To drop my troubles out at the gate.
Making me pause for a moment,
Even when I'm running late.

I can't tell you her name or label,
As she was a piece I randomly struck,
A plant in an old ladies' garden.
Which never flowered where it stood by the hut

Under the shade of others,
She never found the place to be,
But up here, out in the open,
she has been amazing for me.

The old ladies name was Violet,
And I am glad her garden lives on,
In pieces dotted through mine.
They have combined to make their own song.

THE OLDER ROSE

While I have been away, the red rose on my table dehydrated, and I admired how her beauty remains in spite of having no life left in it. This made me think of things ... and this has become the topic of today's poem ...

Love used to be rich and beautiful,
with petals of voluptuous velvet.
Just a bud, which was fresh and new,
Any tears glistened like magical dew.

Drawn to her detailed centre,
Still closed but showing potential.
Curiosity led to distraction.
The colours flooding your imagination

The fragrance was strong and consuming,
And its magic was bright and confusing.
For awhile you forgot your focus,
To be defined and empty, with purpose.

For a moment, engulfed by a rose,
Who twisted the things that you know.
Walls clanged in with practical construction,
to keep busy, cold and directed.

Stepping back, she was left on the table,
Like a long, misinterpreted fable.
Life shifted with clutter, so fast,
And the water dried in her glass.

Over time her edges became brittle,
And the dizziness drifted away.
Her thirst was lost in the desert,
And silence left all to decay.

But her heart still held her shape strong,
And with truth, she remained who she was.
Love cannot be dissolved,
in sensibilities of why and because.

SUNSET

Another day closes,
And another beautiful sky.
As the warmth of light leaves us,
Her colours are trailing behind.
The branches and distant mountains,
Turn from textured to silhouette.
The picture holds us steady,
And creates a time to reflect.
On the moments between the curtains,
The life between dawn and dusk.
The learning and the growing,
The treasures and the troughs.
The glow sinks behind the mountain,
And I breathe the cooling air.
The colours will rise again tomorrow,
With another new story to share.

ALL NIGHT MOON

That beautiful big moon has been up all night.
Drenching her light and keeping the world awake.
The leaves are all face up,
making the most of the extra sustenance.
My seeds, cracking open from their shells,
are reaching up to open their first true leaf.
The wild dogs call from the shadows.
A crisp forest crunches under their paws,
as all the vulnerable bellies are exposed in the branches.
The cobwebs dance in the early morning breeze,
and the diamonds of dew glimmer in the moonlight,
giving away her trap.
The spider waits in the curl of a leaf,
But this evening, her strings remain empty.
The sphere shifts the tides and alters my centre.
I am as moody as those purpling clouds.
Knowing that as she sinks behind the mountain,
the sunrise is painting the day,
and I will be recentred.
Yes, the moon has been up all night and is very late to bed.

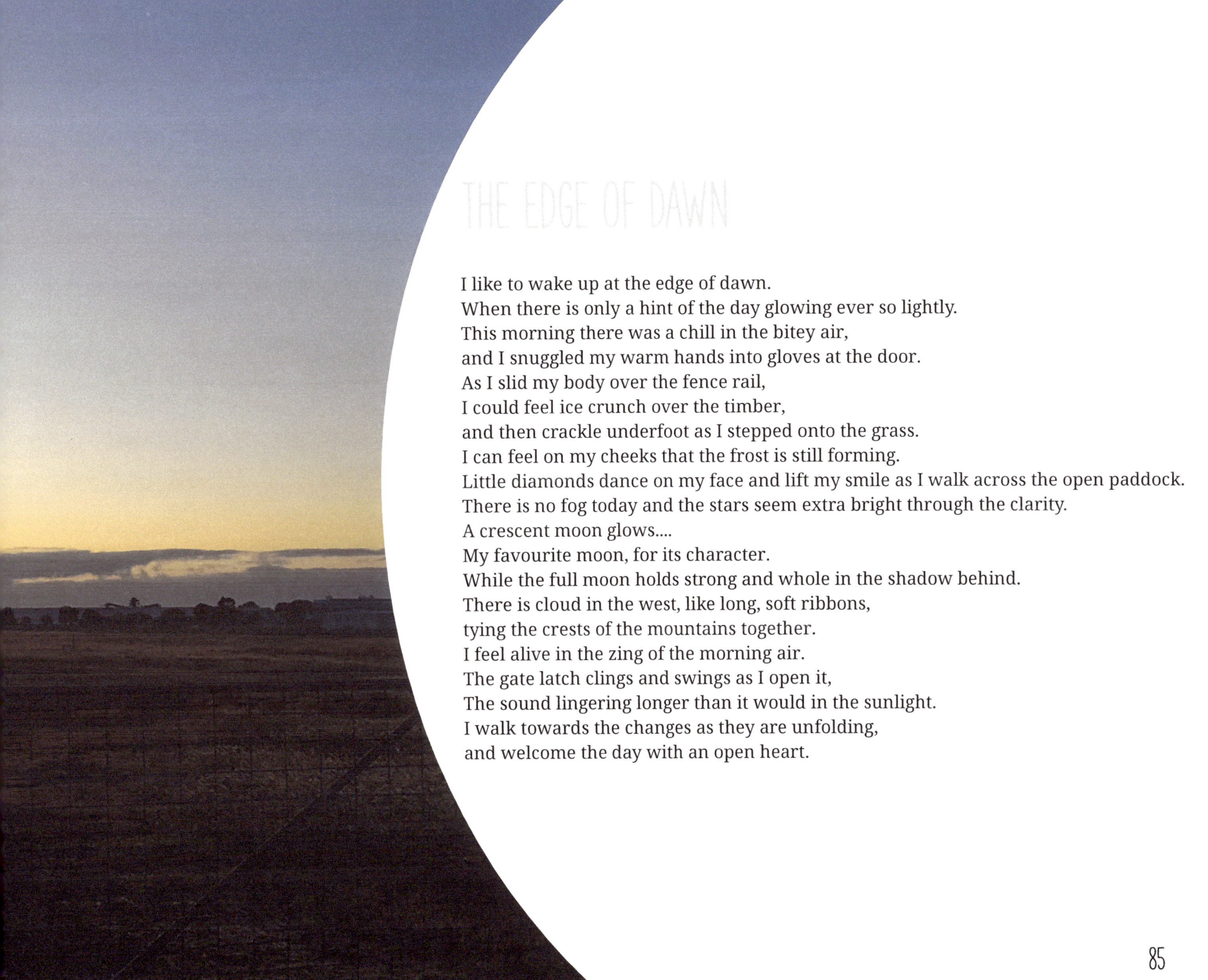

THE EDGE OF DAWN

I like to wake up at the edge of dawn.
When there is only a hint of the day glowing ever so lightly.
This morning there was a chill in the bitey air,
and I snuggled my warm hands into gloves at the door.
As I slid my body over the fence rail,
I could feel ice crunch over the timber,
and then crackle underfoot as I stepped onto the grass.
I can feel on my cheeks that the frost is still forming.
Little diamonds dance on my face and lift my smile as I walk across the open paddock.
There is no fog today and the stars seem extra bright through the clarity.
A crescent moon glows....
My favourite moon, for its character.
While the full moon holds strong and whole in the shadow behind.
There is cloud in the west, like long, soft ribbons,
tying the crests of the mountains together.
I feel alive in the zing of the morning air.
The gate latch clings and swings as I open it,
The sound lingering longer than it would in the sunlight.
I walk towards the changes as they are unfolding,
and welcome the day with an open heart.

CAT'S CLAW MOON?

Cat's claw moon,
A distant tune,
Lambada swinging the distance.

Hesitant ways,
Are lost in a haze,
As attraction smothers resistance.

Silky satin,
Lights like Manhattan,
Reflecting like glowing confetti.

A breeze which tickles,
The tripling ripples,
Lapping the logs of the jetty.

The chill of the air,
We were hot, unaware,
Each breath was holding the moment.

Soft, supple cheeks,
Blush as they meet,
Whispering words as they drift into silence.

The touch of your face,
In a welcome embrace,
Cool nose and gentle lips.

A timeless forever,
Held us together,
I remember the night we first kissed.

CRESCENT MOON

Today, I watched the sunset,
but it was only when it was gone,
that the deeper, richer potion
of the mountains lingered on.
I love a crescent moon.
The shape captures me with her hook.
And draws me towards the darkness
to take another look.
The reflections on the water,
showing twice what I had missed.
The claw upon the water
rippled where it kissed.
The amber colours darkened
to draw a darker hue.
And in the shadows I felt magic,
Like the spark I had with you.

THE SEED

In the beginning you held your hand open.
I was a seed, with my shell and heart broken.
You warmed me in the palm of your hand,
Until I believed you could be my man.

But as I started to open and grow,
I felt your heart harden and close.
The more I have evolved to be yours,
The more reasons you found to dissolve.

Now I think of you walking in the rain,
A bitter wind of hollowness and pain.
I have been trying to sow you my seed,
To fill your centre with everything you need.

But when you feel it, you cast it away,
Like it burns you to feel love in this way
In a puddle I twist at your feet,
Trying to show you how great we could be.

But you hold silent, like I am not even there.
I am confused because I remembered you cared.
You watch me fall away in the water,
Where the chill takes from me, everything tender.

Tumbling down a strong, surging gutter
I know we could have been so much better.
I wonder where the water will take me?
I hope I am grounded before it breaks me.

I long for a warm, open hand,
To show me, he could be my man.

BUYING HAY

The sun was delicious as it touched my skin and garden on the farm today.
Sudo had a fresh bounce of enthusiasm, a game of soccer and even a swim in the dam.
At about 3pm, the air shifts and the ice returns to the gentle breeze.
A signal to me to get rolling on the afternoon routines.
I buy my hay from a dairy farmer over the hill, and as I drive the dirt track towards his driveway, the horizon opens out, broad and wide, bordered by mountains, more distant than the ones I have at home. It is as breathtaking as it is every week, and I am never too familiar to face it with a smile.
The farmer greets me with his cheery grin, the tractor rumbling, awaiting my arrival.
The hay is loaded on the ute, which sinks on its springs with the generous weight.
As we tie it down, we discuss the icy frost of the morning, and the aches in our hands as we crunch and clink our way through the dawn in our morning chores.
I observe a cow in special care, and we discuss how she is travelling, he talks with the fondness you would give a child, as he talks of the importance of proper care and nutrition, right from day one.
One of my ratchet straps is starting to fray, he noticed this last time, and swaps it out with one from the farm.
I head off with the sound of gravel under my tyres, and the evening paints this sweeping colour over the dairy.
I arrive home to a wagging dog who bounces at my side, as I close the door to the hen house, and bring in the wood for this evening's fire.
While sometimes it bites, aches or stings, I do still very much love this lifestyle.
So grateful ❤️

BOUGAINVILLA BIRD

Shy, really. Really, I'm shy.
Though I spike Bouganvillia
Bright on the outside.

Silent in meaning,
My words remain silent.
The singing you hear is a warning cry.

I tuck my head
in my own feather lustre,
My plumage screens my perception.

I wonder what lies,
in the world outside,
But I'm afraid that it's stirred by deception.

In the branches, I'm protected,
From big birds and bad weather,
Though I see a little less sunshine.

Like ears will hear the call,
And if he fits through the thorns,
He must be a bird of my size.

Tawny brown behind colour,
Tiny bird, under cover.
A like mind will discover this centre.

SUN ON SMOKE HAZE

An orange sun sits over my hills in the smoke haze.
Bringing colour to the grey, and beauty to the maze.
I shudder in the centre, while I live on my toes.
For which way it turns, nobody knows.
Reading the wind to be ready for change,
The sun holds me steady in a world, so strange.
Giving me direction with its compass of light.
Bleeding through the darkness as it sinks out of sight.

FIRE ON THE HILLS

After days of evacuation,
Life is on tender-hooks.
Returning to the house, things are cooler and calm.
Spookily quiet really.
In that moment, I wrote this.

I came home today.
As I opened the car door, my lungs filled with smoke.
Obscuring my vision and clouding my thoughts.
Looking down the paddock, I cannot even see the shelters.
My eyes stinging and my thoughts pinging.
My rules for when to leave keep changing like the wind.
But today it is calm and still.
The leaves motionless and the haze sitting heavy on the hills.
All around, my neighbours are prepared.
Special things extracted from their homes and plonked into places where they might survive.
The traffic passes, everyone carrying a trailer,
Like a handkerchief on a stick of their most important treasures.
When we were leaving, my friend said
"Have you got everything?"
I looked at my house before I closed the door and said,
"No, but yes… let's go"

Today I return.
The worst risk has gone, and many have lost.
For us the fire remains, simmering in the background.
Growing by hundreds of hectares every report,
and yet keeping its distance.
Close enough that a change could change everything,
But far enough to question why we are so on edge.
A breath of breeze brings mixed relief to the air,
Shifting the smoke here, but feeding the fire there.
My ears drum to the sound of choppers in a constant passage,
Dulling the active fire edge and targeting the hottest fronts.
Passing so close over the house that I can see what is in their bellies.
My animals and belongings are spread over three houses,
And I am feeling just as scattered.
Poised over every notification as I wait for it to load through a broken internet.
I have been here before.
Being on a wire is exhausting.
Sometimes it takes weeks before the threat really passes.
Always wondering whether we are over reacting or under prepared.
The answer only comes in the future of the way it turns,
Resting in the arms of the weather.
Hanging on a thread pulled by wind directions.
Rain before wind, or wind before rain.
Today I clean my house.
An absurd activity in such conditions,
But I look around and see...
Maybe I don't really need all this stuff.

SUNRISE IN TINTINARA

Sunrise at Tintinara, Breakfast in Bordertown.
I could drive any direction, But I can't turn around.
I travel with a tray of the strangest things
A pot plant, some tea cups and a dragon with wings.
Heading home from Dad's house, that we have to leave empty.
But it's hard to let go of the things that hold memories.
Pockets full of trinkets, which capture his ways,
Swatches of my father in fabric and clay.
I pass through places that I know he knew,
But time spent there together were too far and few.
I stand alone on the banks of a lake,
For having no sleep, I am surprisingly awake.
I look at the ripples, which I imagine we share,
But it's just me and the dog, and we're heading somewhere.
Back in the car, with the windows down.
I hit play on the deck and absorb in the sound.
Compilation discs cut by a friend,
Help reset the road, I'm on my way again.

BRAILLE

I wish I could show you
The book of my verse,
Pull the right cord
To draw your heavy curtains.

What blanked your vision?
Is it reversible blindness?
Do memories close your doors
or bring colours to darkness?

My words stay invisible
As they dissolve, black on black.
Frustration in myself
for I can't write braille.

Enter the covers,
There's more senses that one.
The most you will bleed
is a paper cut thumb.

I write with definition,
The bound edges display me.
When ink hits the paper,
I press the page firmly.

Touch my words with your fingers,
Let your print feel the impression.
If your heart is sensitive,
You just might feel them.

THE WALL

You say that your heart was extinguished,
By a storm that blew it all out.
You say that there is nothing left,
But when we touch, that is something I doubt.

I see a big steel wall,
Which crashed down to protect your centre.
It is strong, and thick, and heavy,
And could hold your heart clear forever.

But through it are tiny holes,
Which show me right into your heart.
When I see how warmly it glows,
The ache just tears me apart.

I trace the holes, so lightly,
Hoping I won't cause further damage,
I would love to lift the wall clear,
But it takes a strength I can't manage.

I wish I could blow away the cloud,
That exploded into the storm.
I had a cloak of hurt and fear,
Which drove me to a path, well worn.

I know that we could get through
Without clouds, cloaks or walls.
Behind our means of protection,
Is a love that could pass through them all.

If I help you lift this wall,
Can you help me shed the cloud.
With trust and communication,
We can build on this magic we've found.

THE TIDAL LAGOON

You shift like a tidal lagoon,
And it's hard to know where I stand.
Sometimes I am in over my head,
But sometimes I'm out on dry land.

Sometimes your water is so fresh,
It quenches my every need.
It shimmers so clearly around me,
In a way that lets me believe.

It rises through my cheeks, I am smiling.
As it sings through all that I know.
My old crooked soul seems like it's new again.
I feel alive as I am washed by your flow.

But sometimes your water is salty.
You sting me with every cut.
But it's a hurt that I can feel healing,
And that allows me to open right up.

Your truth is so direct, it dives into my canyons.
And that lays bare my pain.
But your brine closes all of my bleeding,
and soon I feel whole again.

I can feel your care holding beneath me.
I am in suspension, so I let myself float.
But your tide is changing again,
And I have to get back on my toes.

Sometimes you pull right away,
And all that is left is your mud.
I get tangled in the roots of your mangroves,
And those days aren't so much fun.

Sometimes we pause in a moment;
It feels steady, and I can feel brave,
But then suddenly the water is receding,
And you disappear, and go with a wave.

I know that I can't lock you in.
I understand your need to flow.
I try to just bend with the current,
But sometimes I don't know which way to go.

It is hard to dive in to our passion,
When I am not sure which depth I will find.
So I try to drift with your variations,
And hope my place will evolve with time.

Photo: Dana Ashlakoff

This morning was a magnificent morning.

A wide thick rainbow nestled its feet in the gully between my mountains. The sky was a misty grey and gold warmed the flanks of the dark blue hills. Stopping my feet for a moment, and taking my breath away before disappearing into the cloud.

I walked along the forest edge and something scuttled under the bracken and disappeared between the maze of mossy trunks and spikey branches.

I continued on my way, no pictures taken today.

But by the time I got to the top of the hill, I had written today's poem..
.

THE SHADOW

Because it was only a flicker,
I couldn't tell if you were a fox or a bird.
All you gave me was a shadow,
So the feelings I have are absurd.
Perhaps my sunshine was too much for you,
My breeze, a little too strong.
I saw you ducking for cover,
Before I could let out a song.
Your footprint stays on my centre,
Even though you were passing through.
I won't try to catch or hold you,
Because that just wouldn't be true.
So you fly on, into your own world
And I absorb into mine.
If this was supposed to be something.
I guess I will see you sometime.

HAPPY NEW YEAR

At the close of a year,
And the close of the day,
We look back in reflection
At who we became.

The things that we gained,
And those that we lost.
The choices we made,
And what was the cost?

How we reacted,
And how we behaved.
When we were weak,
And when we were brave.

The things that went right,
And the things that went wrong.
Things we should have seen coming
And known all along.

But the times that were different,
And not as we thought,
Brought surprises of heart,
Where our emotions were caught.

These are the times,
when we grow the most,
Stepping outside of our comfort zone.
Let love in the crevices,

Where you thought it was gone.
Let butterflies play where they don't belong.
Do not cling to the history and make it repeat.
Test new ground with soft bare feet.

Pick the eyes from your learning and sew them into the dawn.
Let them take shape without holding on
Each day we wake up, is to be grateful of life.
Knowing each time we awaken, just a little more wise.

STRETCHED TAUT

When your eyes are all big and bleary,
And your insides are squishing, all teary.
When systems fall crashing around you,
And disasters come forth to astound you.

When your elastic squeaks with the stretching,
Just remember that life's only testing.
You may feel like you will snap into fragments,
But trust, you'll eventually make it.

The effort wins with persistence.
Each test builds another resistance.
The trapeze swings high at the circus,
But the rush of the flight makes it worth it.

THE CLIFF TO ASPIRATION

Toes on the lip
Of a perfect desire.
I can feel the rush, and I'm still on the edge.

On the verge of lifting
Away from the soil,
Which has always been my grounding.

The skin of my feet
Divides on the risk,
decision cuts my soles like a razor.

My centre is custard,
Quivering yellow,
It has always been safe and guarded.

My stomach dissolves
And cringes in my ribs,
But even my bones won't save me.

Blind my conscience
Of reason and logic.
Hold level to settle the flinching.

Rinsing away
Practical thinking,
Diluting my fears to subliminal.

Cast off these lines
which tie me to the shore,
Take a raw slice of the dare.

Pursuit of the flesh
is a gameful test,
Drive is the key to the Valiant.

Compelled by adventure,
But shivering deeply.
Can I crack this case into courage?

Will I have the endurance
To follow it through?
Only leaping will unknot this wrangle.

I held the white feather,
But it blew from my wings,
So, I am left with bare empty palms.

The cliff screens no hedging,
Just a strong open wind.
I need to launch into where it comes from.

Breathe in the air
Which blows from my destiny,
Close the door on the cage of the craven.

It's time to launch
Into the reckless unknown,
And trust in the future which shapes me.

VALENTINE'S DAY

We are all driven by love and fear.
Fear of hurt that makes us brittle to the core,
Reactive and judgmental.
Predicting pain which then makes pain inevitable.

The strength of love makes us empowered,
A magic that can lift us through anything.
A nutrition that fills our core.

Being mindful of our own fears, and the fears of others,
Helps us to softly rest love in its place.
Be soft when you face the spikes of fear.

In searching for the perfect love, the one we wish we had,
We can forget to appreciate the love we already have.
Not just the love of a partner,
but also, the love of our family, friends, animals,
And the environment that carries our life.

Love unconditionally, and with all of your heart,
And open your soul to it's magic.
Happy Valentine's Day ❤️

MORNING TIME

When my alarm goes off, it is dark...
I lie there and I think to myself.
"Why am I getting up so early?"
The air feels cold on my face,
and I feel snuggly among the pillows.
I hear a light tip-tap of claws on a wooden floor,
followed by the flapping of Sudo's ears against her face.
A familiar sound, as she shakes last nights dreams from her foggy head,
clearing the way for another enthusiastic day.
Stretching in the doorway,
she reminds me that I should do the same.
I hear the bray of a donkey call across the hills
as he reminds me that it is almost time for breakfast.
A soft pink glow very gently warms the walls,
And I realize that I am late to greet the day.
Sudo welcomes me with a hug, a moment for love.
and then we head into the paddocks for today's adventures.

A Touch from Aphrodite

The evening draws dark,
And the day was long.
Your amble is slow and weighted.

Settle your swag
And sink into sleep.
Let starlight refreshen your purpose.

I've been watching you travel
Through roads rough and twisted.
I flinched with your every stumble.

If you let me touch you,
I could salt and cleanse you.
From here, I just feel the pain.

My hand is beneath you,
Though you never feel it.
Trust it's hold if you need a soft landing.

You will travel as yourself,
But my desire is to lift you.
The strength of my love makes you light in my palms.

Let me sink through within,
From your centre to skin.
Let me be the spell which heals you.

Your direction is valued,
Your honesty and virtue,
Rest now in a blanket of serenity.

In your silent sleep,
I bathe your worn feet.
When you wake again, I'll be invisible.

MELLIFLUOUS

He said that she was mellifluous,
As she chortled her words like a creek.
Laughter bounced through her energy,
As she tickled the world with her leaves.

She fluttered through the sky, like a butterfly.
And danced on the tips of her toes.
When she dreamed of magical wishes,
She would wriggle the end of her nose.

Her words rolled out, like a melody,
And tingled the air, like a song
She warmed the heart of the cabin,
And rested like she belonged.

She came in waves, like the ocean,
And could easily burst into a storm,
But even with thunder and lightning,
The sunshine would glisten, so warm.

Her love was rich, like honey,
As she sparkled with cheek in her eyes,
But her wings were broad, like an eagle,
And needed to be open, to fly.

www.ingramcontent.com/pod-product-compliance
Lightning Source LLC
Chambersburg PA
CBHW042106090526

44590CB00004B/114